T0120897

GRANT IT UNTO ME DEAR LORD

Doris Wesley Bettis

HE IS RISEN

Doris Wesley Bettis

Doris Wesley- Bettis

HE LOVED ME SO

Doris Wesley Bettis

God gave to us His

on - ly Son and through His death the bat-tle's fought and won They cru - ci fied my

Lord on Cal - va-ry Oh how He bled — and died for you and me! He

HE WILL GIVE YOU PEACE, PEACE, PEACE

Doris Wesley Bettis

HOW
(How Can I Give Thanks)

Doris Wesley Bettis

I'M FILLED WITH PRAISE

Doris Wesley Bettis

I NEED THE WORD OF GOD

Doris Wesley Bettis

Doris Wesley- Bettis

34

I REALLY LOVE THE LORD

Doris Wesley Bettis

LET JESUS ABIDE

Doris Wesley Bettis

side_____ Glo-ry glo-ry hal-le-lu — jah_____ Let Je-sus a - bide_____
stirred_____

___ Let His Name be e - ver - last - ing_____ for the Lord is on our

side_____ Shout it out____ to the side

NEW HEAVEN

Doris Wesley Bettis

Hea ven_   a New   Hea ven_   Hea ven_   For the for-mer things - are

passed - a - way   A Ho-ly Ci-ty   New Jer - u-sa-lem com ing down

NO THEY WON'T FIND HIM

Doris Wesley Bettis

44

STOP BY LORD

Doris Wesley Bettis

stop by now   Oh   stop by now   Oh   stop by now   Oh   stop by now

Some-bod-y needs   one   touch from You Lord   Oh   stop   by   Lord - Stop by____

THAT NAME JESUS

Doris Wesely Bettis

Soloist: That name Je - sus   It

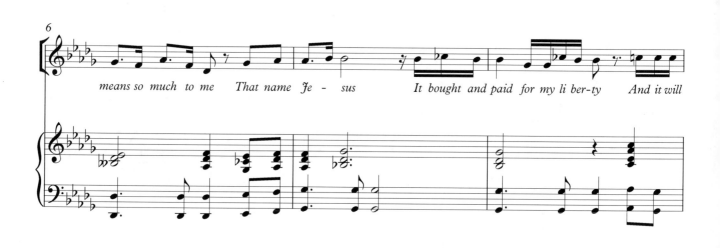

means so much to me   That name Je - sus   It bought and paid for my li ber-ty   And it will

chase a thou-sand that Name — and I — — That name Je - sus   My

THE BLOOD OF JESUS

Doris Wesley Bettis

Doris Wesley- Bettis

54

THE LORD IS MY SHEPHERD

Doris Wesley Bettis

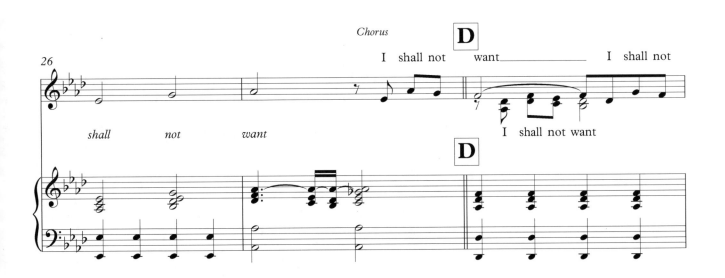

THIS IS THE DAY

Doris Wesley Bettis

WELL DONE

Doris Wesley Bettis

Doris Wesley- Bettis

Printed in the United States
By Bookmasters